Shark Bites

Mako Shark

by Jenna Lee Gleisner

Bullfrog Books

Ideas for Parents and Teachers

Bullfrog Books let children practice reading informational text at the earliest reading levels. Repetition, familiar words, and photo labels support early readers.

Before Reading

- Discuss the cover photo. What does it tell them?

- Look at the picture glossary together. Read and discuss the words.

Read the Book

- "Walk" through the book and look at the photos. Let the child ask questions. Point out the photo labels.

- Read the book to the child, or have him or her read independently.

After Reading

- Prompt the child to think more. Ask: Mako sharks look a lot like great white sharks. What similar features do they have?

Bullfrog Books are published by Jump!
5357 Penn Avenue South
Minneapolis, MN 55419
www.jumplibrary.com

Library of Congress Cataloging-in-Publication Data

Names: Gleisner, Jenna Lee, author.
Title: Mako shark / by Jenna Lee Gleisner.
Description: Bullfrog books edition. | Minneapolis, MN : Jump!, Inc., [2020]
Series: Shark bites | Includes bibliographical references and index.
Audience: Age 5-8. | Audience: K to Grade 3.
Identifiers: LCCN 2019001200 (print)
LCCN 2019002852 (ebook)
ISBN 9781641289665 (ebook)
ISBN 9781641289658 (hardcover : alk. paper)
Subjects: LCSH: Mako sharks—Juvenile literature.
Classification: LCC QL638.95.L3 (ebook)
LCC QL638.95.L3 G545 2020 (print) DDC 597.3/3—dc23
LC record available at https://lccn.loc.gov/2019001200

Editors: Susanne Bushman and Jenna Trnka
Design: Shoreline Publishing Group

Photo Credits: Saulty725/Dreamstime, cover, 5, 23bl; Lukas Walter/Shutterstock, 1, 3; wildestanimal/Shutterstock, 4, 6–7, 8, 10–11, 23tl; Linda Johnsonbaugh/Dreamstime, 6, 23br; Martin Prochazkacz/Shutterstock, 9, 14–15; Saulty725/Shutterstock, 12–13, 18–19; Andrea Izzotti/Shutterstock, 16, 23tr; Paulo Oliveira/Alamy, 17; NaturePL/SuperStock, 20–21; Prochym/Adobe Stock, 22; Mark Kostich/Shutterstock, 24.

Printed in the United States of America at Corporate Graphics in North Mankato, Minnesota.

Table of Contents

Fast Shark

See these eyes?

Big.

Black.

snout

Long teeth.

A pointed snout.

A torpedo shape.
What is this?
A mako shark!
Nice!

torpedo

Its top is dark.

Its belly is white.

gills

It swims.

It never stops.

Why?

Water flows
over its gills.

It breathes!

It is the
fastest shark!

How fast?

Up to 60 miles
(97 kilometers)
per hour!

Wow!

It swims far.

How far?

About 36 miles
(58 km) a day!

It is smart.

It hunts prey.

Like what?

Fish.

16

Even swordfish!
Neat!

swordfish

17

Zoom!
It swims.
Wow!

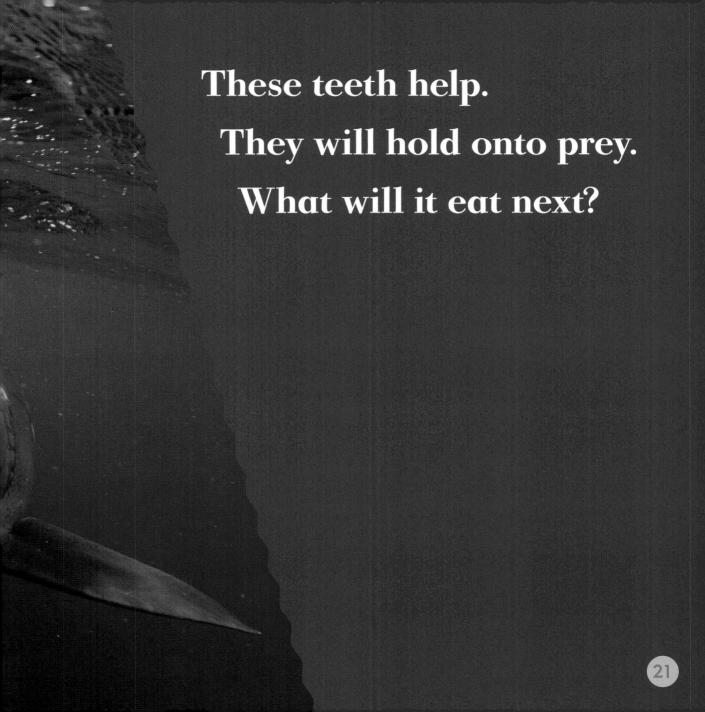

These teeth help.
They will hold onto prey.
What will it eat next?

Parts of a Mako Shark

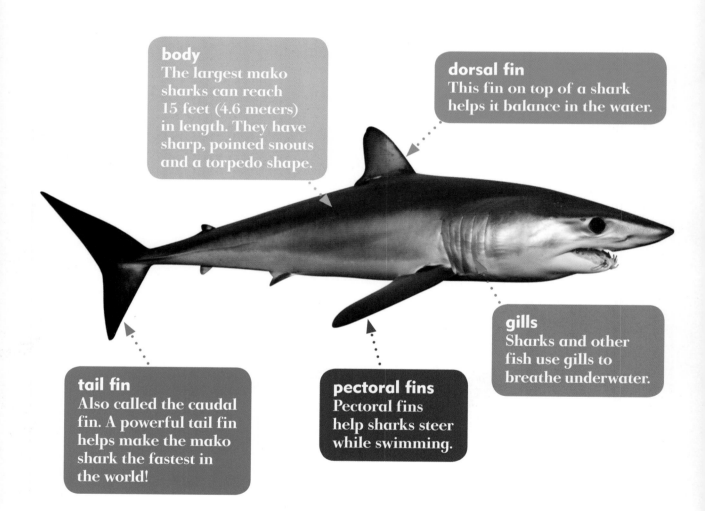

body
The largest mako sharks can reach 15 feet (4.6 meters) in length. They have sharp, pointed snouts and a torpedo shape.

dorsal fin
This fin on top of a shark helps it balance in the water.

gills
Sharks and other fish use gills to breathe underwater.

tail fin
Also called the caudal fin. A powerful tail fin helps make the mako shark the fastest in the world!

pectoral fins
Pectoral fins help sharks steer while swimming.

Picture Glossary

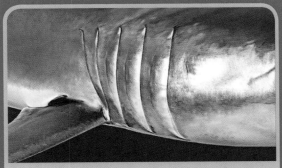

gills
Organs near a fish's mouth through which it breathes by extracting oxygen from water.

prey
Animals that are hunted by other animals for food.

snout
The long front part of an animal's head that includes the nose, mouth, and jaws.

torpedo
A thin, pointed, cylinder-shaped underwater device.

Index

To Learn More

Finding more information is as easy as 1, 2, 3.

❶ Go to www.factsurfer.com

❷ Enter "makoshark" into the search box.

❸ Choose your book to see a list of websites.